All My Random Thoughts in a Book

All My Random Thoughts in a Book

Jewell Coleman

Conviction 2 Change LLC
www.conviction2change.com

All My Random Thoughts in a Book by Jewell Coleman

Edition 2018

Copyright © 2018 Jewell Coleman

Published by Conviction 2 Change LLC
PO Box 47 Daly City, CA 94016
www.conviction2change.com

Library Congress Control Number: 2018956463
ISBN: 1732712115
ISBN-13: 9781732712119

Illustration: Inara Quliyeva
IG: @inarina_illustration

Cover Design: Kayla N. Lott

Editor: Taylor D. Duckett
IG: @C2Cpublishing
Conviction2change@outlook.com

Acknowledgements

First, I want to thank God for helping me get through all these obstacles, obstacles that helped shape me to be the person that I am today. Without Him I am nothing.

Thanks to my sister MyKia Coleman for encouraging to stop hiding my poems, to share them with the world, and for always having a listening ear when I needed it the most.

Thanks to my Father and Mother, Michael and Kena Coleman for always supporting me and encouraging me through the different phases that I go through in life.

Thank you to Inara Quliyeva, all the way from Finland, for taking time out of her busy schedule to design such a lovely illustration for me. Follow her @inarina_illustration on Instagram. She's the best and is an amazing artist!

Thank you to Kayla N. Lott for putting the finishing touches on such a creative, beautiful cover! She is a fantastic designer!

Thanks to my cousin, Nantambu Fentress, for introducing me to Conviction 2 Change LLC without hesitation. Check out his book, "Faith and Follow – Through: A Dream Conquered."

Thank you to Conviction 2 Change LLC for giving me a chance to put all of my random thoughts in a book, and for publishing my first work.

#Throwback to The Fun Times

Seems just like yesterday
I was holding you & laughing
all in your face.

I go through different phases,
you must accept
that I'm always evolving & changing.

I Have Different Needs

You can't play with me like you did everybody else.
I flowed through you like water in a creek,
but somehow you drowned me.

At This Point, What Is Life?

I don't know what I want,
'cause the one I thought I wanted
made me feel so unwanted...

sigh

It's a black & white world,
but with you I glow iridescent.

Breaking FREE

I was that girl that always thought highly of everyone else
but doubted herself.
The girl that saw the universe in everyone else
but never saw the universe in herself.

I was the girl that always wanted to be me,
but was too afraid they'd judge me.
The girl that saw me as just a me
instead of glorifying my uniqueness
& how special I was to be.

 I was the girl that simply wanted to be
free, loving & everything in between.

Me.
That's all I ever wanted to be.

Me & The Universe Became One

I finally realized that there's more to life
than just "YOU & ME."
I found a universe that was filled with love,
acceptance & heartwarming things.
I thought it was a dream,
because lately I haven't been feeling a thing.
I opened up to things that made me feel loved,
& figured out that all I ever needed was me
& the man above.

My Heart Led Me to A Heartbreak

I always told myself
you would one day be the face of a stranger.
I knew that one day you'd put my heart in danger.
I just didn't know that it would be that soon,
I didn't know that I'd be left with nothing
but a mouth full of words to say to you.
I didn't think you'd hurt me that way.
I was wishful thinking hoping you'd somehow feel my pain,
& somehow see that I wanted you to stay.

He Was Tripping

He had me feeling like
I wasn't worthy enough to commit to.

To: J.B.

Is it weird for me to say that I still got shy when I thought of you & your face?
Remember how we chilled, watched movies & sipped wine on my couch?
I thought we were at least getting somewhere instead you stopped coming around.

> Is it weird for me to say that I still wanted you even though I knew you'd never stay?

I remember those Saturday nights we'd go to random places, playing & laughing all night.

> Is it weird for me to say that when you disappeared out of my life, no matter the years, I always waited for you to show up or reappear?

When you finally did, I had to act like I've been doing fine & like I didn't want you near.

> Is it safe to say that out of everyone, you're my favorite mistake?

'Cause every year I missed your hands, your presence & your smile.
I thought of you EVERYDAY, 365 DAYS, but I knew you'd NEVER STAY.
I was a fool to even allow myself to keep thinking that way.
You never deserved my time nor my attention.

> Can't believe I tried to get you to fill that position.

In an All-Time Rewind

I forget the things that I'm dying to remember
and remember the things that I'm dying to forget.
Life's backwards.
I'm backwards.

The Same Mentality

Maybe it's your persistence that scares me.
I've never had someone stick around this long
even after consistently pushing them away.

Maybe it's your consistency that scares me,
because it's always me putting in all the work
while others
fall off,
become distant
& move on without me.

Maybe it's your attention that scares me,
you actually listen to my every word,
even if it's just me reminiscing
or talking crazy.

Maybe it's my feelings that scare me,
because for once I can say
I've connected with a person
that actually felt the same connection.

Maybe it scares me
because I'm done with being scared
& I think I'm ready to give you all of me...
maybe.

I Prayed & Prayed

I remember there was a day
when I prayed to not feel a thing.
My heart had become numb,
I didn't know what else to do or say.

I remember there was a day
when I prayed for the pain
I brought upon myself to go away.
The pain, too heavy to carry,
was showing on my face.

I remember there was a day
When I realized that solitude
was my best choice
& my only happy place.

I remember these things
like it was just yesterday.

The Corny Virgin Truth

The more I show interest,
all they want to do is give me inches.
I want more than that.

I want to know you,
learn you
observe you.

I want to know you more than the word MORE.
I want to know you so well
if I were to ever go blind
by the feel & tracing of your hands & body
I would no doubt know it's you.

I want to know you so well
if we went out to eat
I could order food for you.
Or if you're rushing
I could pick out an outfit
I know you'd love.

I want to know you so deeply
that knowing you
is also loving you.

I don't want your money
or material things
I simply want more
of you.

My Cyclical Lifestyle

I can't digest my thoughts or actions anymore.
Everything is like a big white cloud
or maybe, more like a blur.

My thoughts confuse me,
feelings manipulate me,
my heart leads me astray.

My mind is scrambled
keeping me going
in a never-ending cycle.

"Help"
my soul screamed,
feeling every broken feeling,
remembering every hurtful memory

PSA: Leave Me Alone

I'd rather be a loner,
'cause I can't find no one real,
real enough to stick around
& make me stronger.
I'm not trying to feel no more pain,
I'm just trying to heal.
'Cause these people nowadays act the same.
Always phony & switching up on me.

Simple but Meaningful

I don't want to change you,
I just see a better you.
I'm always looking deeper.

Loner Life, The Best Life

I've gotten used to hanging out alone
being solo dolo.
Hanging out with others
feels hella awkward.

I'd rather go back home.

Expired Time

When I say I don't have time for relationships anymore,
what I mean is I don't have time for:
meaningless texts,
calls,
& FaceTimes.
Those "Come Thru, just so I can use you because I'm
lonely" type of people.

I don't have time for useless dates & indecisiveness,
I don't have time to fall for someone
only to end up
landing flat on my face,
drowning in the deepest parts of my emotions.

I don't have time for:
"maybe,"
"I think so,"
"I'm not sure."

I don't have time to waste any more time.

I can't see myself opening up
letting my walls down
only to end up wishing
I would've built them
1,000,000,000 feet higher.

I know its selfish for me to be this way,
but every time I try
it always ends the same.

Maybe I'm the one to blame,
but then again,
I could very well say
you guys *made* me this way.

I'm not completely writing off relationships.
I'm MORE CAUTIOUS,
caring for ME
& my MENTAL HEALTH.

Me, Myself & My Vibes ONLY

Just me,

without a crew.

I'm too

COMFORTABLE

in
my

SOLITUDE.

Don't Hit My Line With That Foolery

Never understood
why people felt so comfortable
with putting me in the
"option"
or "let me hit her up 'cause I'm bored" category.

Whenever their main chick is tripping
they come to me.
I never gave them the impression
that I was willing to take the "sideline" position!

My "I'm available" is no longer available!

I don't see why people always try to latch on to me
& keep me on standby.
as if I can carry their weight & mine so seemingly?
I'm reminded why
I keep my walls up high.
Still a loner
I shove people away
rather than listening to them.

It's all

FAKE!

You Are Special, You Are Worth It

Alright, ALRIGHT!
Enough of you not thinking you're enough, it's
time to smother yourself in a plethora of self-love.

Remember This

Pretty skies still arise
after darkness filled nights

The Repetitive Truth

Ever since the one I wanted didn't want me,
I've been curving everyone that comes around.

Ever since the one I wanted didn't want me,
I've been distant, not even trying to speak.

Ever since the one I wanted didn't want me,
I've quit trying to connect with people,
too afraid they'd play me.

Ever since the one I wanted didn't want me,
I've chosen to be alone
so that I can love me.

Earthly Sounds

When it's raining outside
I like to listen to the rain drops hit the earth
instead of the thoughts in my head.

My Mouthful, Candid Rant

I'm at the stage in my life where I just want to be left alone.

As lonely as I am,
I want to remain in my solitude
until I figure out my purpose.
I have no room in my heart or mind
to open up to someone.
I have no room for people to come in my life temporarily.

I have no more room
for limited relationships, meaningless text messages
& FaceTime calls.
I'm searching for inner-peace & my destiny.

I can't afford to lose myself within someone
that only intends to drain me
& use me as an option.
I'm tired of being tired & stagnant.

I just want positive progress
mentally,
physically,
emotionally.

I want success,
to be a better me in all aspects of my life.

I've been dealing with the same things for years now.
I'm evolving
for self-love,

self-assurance,
self-awareness
& self-patience.

I need to know
if I never find someone to love,
I already have & hold all the love
I'll ever want & need.

Time is ticking.
The older I get the more fragile I'm becoming.
What comes with being fragile?
Gentleness.
I need care, love & affection
I no longer have the energy or mental space for puppy love,
long talks that only lead to long goodbyes.

I need a life that's full
of love,
happiness,
joy,
peace,
balance
& weird, fun memories.

I need freedom.
I need a new aroma that's filled with all the things
I am afraid to be.

I need a new atmosphere of acceptance & greetings.
I need a new world to come & swallow me whole.
So that I can be me & allow myself to be free.

A space filled with stars, fluffy clouds & happy places.
A place filled with positive guidance
influencing me to go to the highest dimensions
I am afraid to evolve to.
I need vibey views to enter my life
so that I might have peace
& a happy smile with gratitude.

This life has been hell & a half.

One day I'll sit back & laugh, realizing that where I was, was
only taking me to where I am going.

My Solitude Defined Me.

My Love

I stepped out of my solitude
just to be here with you,
darling, you are special.

Stuck & Sinking

I'm a memory keeper.
No wonder why
I can't let you
or anything else
go.

Be Soft, Be You

I've concluded
I'm a compassionate, sensitive, emotional person.
I've grown to accept it.
I feel everything deeply
That's what makes me *me*.
What makes me *glow*.

Society makes us feel that if we're soft
we're weak,
cheesy & clingy.

In my eyes,
if you're soft
you have a heart,
you are forgiving
& hold a warmth
that could warm & mend
the coldest hearts.

Y'all can change & act heartless if you want.
I'm going to stay soft, loving, caring.

This world needs more people like me.

Positivity Matters

In a world where evil is on the rise,
you have to be
love,
peace,
kind,
& on your own side.

How Dare You

How dare you be cold
  when life itself is pure love

How dare you be cold
  when life offers us love in the weirdest but
  purest forms

How dare you be cold
  when breathing & living is love

How dare you be cold
  when seeing the sunset & moon is a breathtaking
  love in itself

How dare you be cold
  in a world full of vibrant colors that welcome us in
  by making us feel loved

Isolation at Its Finest

I was unsure about my position on this earth,
unsure about your position in my life.
Instead of trying to figure everything out,
I decided to isolate myself.

Keep Your Secrets A Secret

YIKESS!!!!
I've opened up to a guy that made me feel comfortable
with knowing my worst sides.
I told him my deepest, darkest memories.
I'm starting to regret all of it.
Why is my life like this?

#SoDraining

Unsureness

I'm unsure about everything in my life
my friends, my feelings, my emotions,
my way of thinking, my being, my existence,
my dreams.
What a scary place to be.

#InANonchalantMood

Better Believe That

I choose to be anti-social for a reason. Everyone doesn't deserve to get to know the real me, my flaws, my love, my personality, my jokes, my slang, my insecurities or the way I think.

My vibes are way too special to just give & share with any & everyone. I refuse to show a seasonal person my small majestic world that I went through hell & back to build, maintain & stay sane while surrounded by pure insanity.

Only to give them the authority to pick & choose if they want to be a part of it or not. I am not just a gem or a ruby you find in some old treasure chest, I am a JEWELL & that's something that you will RESPECT!

Hold On, Don't Give Up

We are all beautiful human beings
dealing with ugly situations

To: My Sister Kia

You're blooming because
you survived the rain.

I Love You, keep it up.
You're doing GREAT!

Fed Up, Yet Still Trying

The older I get the more my life falls apart;
my dreams seem further away.
The more good I do
the more bad I get in return.

I sometimes feel like giving up.

I'm tired of trying only to end up being disappointed.
I'm tired of loving only to feel hated.
I'm tired of trying to mend when I'm constantly broken.
I'm tired of smiling when inside I'm frowning.
I'm tired of searching & not finding.
I'm tired of everything being so twisted & confusing.

I never thought that life could break you down to your last
& even then keep breaking you
until you are minced into pieces.
Instead of being pure & full
you're drained & dried up;
it's insanity.

I'm done with this foolery.

NO Attachments

Not trying to get attached,
because I know once I'm latched
it always backfires.
I end up being the only one hurt.
It wouldn't be right
if I wasn't the one left in confusion.

Lost But Found

Running from love yet searching for it.
Saying, "this is the last time"
yet giving people multiple chances.
Screaming, "I HATE THIS,"
yet growing to love it more & more.
How do you process
when everything you thought you understood
has confused you?

Used to It All

I don't know about anything anymore...

Balance

I don't want you to stay
if my unbalanced lifestyle drains you,
if my insecurities show up a little too much.
If you can balance me that would be lovely.
I'd appreciate that very much.

Maybe I'll Know One Day

Maybe you're right,
maybe all of you are right.
Maybe I don't know what I want.
Maybe I'm still finding myself
and that's why I can't find
the one that's quite to my liking.
Maybe I don't know what I truly like.
Maybe when I find myself
I'll find you.
Maybe I'll find my other half.

Until then I'll remain in my solitude,
fighting for dear life,
trying to run away from this loneliness.
Crying every night to digest this chaos in my life.
I'll keep taking it step by step.
One deep breath after the other.
One day after another.

#HopelessRomanceWhileInSolitude

Holding on to the Wrong One

The day I get over you,
will be the day I get back my life & mind.
I'm numb to my feelings,
except for the ones I have for you.
Feelings are like poison,
& so are you.

To: YOU

I've been having hurtful withdrawals from you for years.
You chose to be inconsistent & distant.
It caused my heart to be sickened.
I told you I wasn't going to play these games;
you insisted that I play.
You could sense that I was new to love.
I'm still recovering
while you're out hanging with your old boo.

To: B.R.

I know you're running low on patience with me.
I know you're tired of waiting on me to
    let go
        & let you in.

I know you're fed up with my indecisive
       actions, texts, calls, & paragraphs.

I know I'm confusing & misleading at times.
I truly apologize,
I'm completely scattered
emotionally,
    physically,
        mentally.

I can't quite understand
my emotions,
    thoughts,
       & my wishful thinking love life.

"I'm trying" my heart whispered.

Chained

You want to know something?
I tried to do what I normally do with you with him.
I tried laying on his chest,
listening to his heart beat.
playing with his hands,
pointing out the stars & moon to him.
I tried laughing at his jokes,
but they weren't as funny.
I even tried starting little convos,
but it didn't feel right.
It actually felt like
nothing.
I look for you in everyone I meet now.
I still can't fathom what you've done to me.
I HATE every bit of it.

Been There Done That, But Still Here

What is there to feel
When you feel like
You've felt it all?

Self vs Self

save me from ME
lately I've been living in a dream
thinking about everything
feeling so many feelings
but not understanding a thing

Mend & Move On

Living broken isn't living
only surviving

A Mind Check

Your mind will wander as far as you let it.
Let it.
It's okay to be wondrous & open minded,
but don't let it wander too far.
Have it in control
before it sneaks up & controls you.

Life is A Mess, A Gorgeous Mess

If you let it, life can take you to dark enclosed places
& leave you there to build yourself back up,
time & time again.

You're weaker, but still crawling back up to the surface
trying to save yourself again.
With all the scratches, bruises & scars
reminding you that what you thought destroyed you
helped you survive.

Sometimes we have to go insane to find our sanity

Life's a roller coaster going in a huge circle,
not the perfect circle that you see in geometry or art.
But a circle that seems perfect & crisp
but has hidden swirls, squares & rectangles.

Life's all about good & bad surprises
never get too comfortable with things going well.
As soon as you think life's great,
something bad will creep in
& try to destroy everything,
if you let it

Always stay alert but calm.
The prettiest lips say the prettiest lies,
the softest roses have the hardest thorns,
the darkest times have the brightest endings
the sweetest smiles go through the most bitter times.

Life is backwards, accept it, learn from it
don't be blind to it.

Open your eyes
even your spiritual one.

The Cliché Truth

You have to be comfortable with being by yourself,
before you allow yourself to open up
& be with someone else.

Another "L" Taken

I knew exactly what I was getting myself into
when I decided to hang out with you
now I'm the one left with all the hurt
I guess I thought I could change you,
maybe I took it too far.

US

Penetrate my heart
while I penetrate your mind
Let's grow in love
Let's be pure and divine

Life is More So Taking Than Giving

When life offers you something
whether BIG or small,
Cherish it with all your being,
for life isn't too giving.

My Comfort

Out of all the places I like to go
you're my HAPPY place.

HURT, HURT, HURT, HURT

I'm at a sad place in my life
I can't quite pin point
where the hurt is coming from.
There's so much destruction
I don't know what's destroying me most.

Love War

Unraveling myself from you is painful
I'm constantly going back & forth because of you

Seeking Warmth

many nights I went to sleep freezing
because of my frozen blue heart
trying to warm my heart
with candles, incense & love poems
one day I'll be warm again
not because of you
but because of self-love.

Illusion

soon could be forever
& *forever*
could be...*never*

I Hope You Knew This

I'm not gonna say *"I Love You"*
because it's too early
but I will say I adore you &
I want your presence to stay forever

Empty

225 days until winter;
I don't think I'm ready for the cold weather,
I seem to feel even more lonely in winter than any season.
The way the leaves fall, the wind blows,
the way the moon sits so gloomy in the sky
only reminds me of how empty I really feel
for once I want to feel whole
for a whole year.

My Life, My Life

I'm tired & drained,
with no clue what's my next step in life
I'm just living day to day
wondering but not thinking
alive but not feeling
lonely but not pondering.
I'm physically just here
breathing, trying, failing, trying, failing, trying, failing.
Being inconsistent & distant
hoping that one day someone will stop
& listen to my thoughts, ideas, my dreams.

knowing me,
I'm too freaking shy to pull out the real me
Not to mention how anti-social I am
It's been a tough lil teenage life
constantly hyping myself up to start
but never consistent
feeling like my time is being wasted
I should've just continued.
Maybe, I would have seen results.

WOW

I never thought I'd meet someone
stingy enough
to put a limit on our forever.

Mentally Bonding

You opened my mind in ways that I'd never imagined
I catch myself gazing at the stars saying,
"Man, this is amazing."
How one human being can open up another's mind
with a select few words with so much depth
It's *magic!*
I don't want to lose this feeling
Stay.
I love it.
I Love You.

Forgive Yourself

I had to sit back
& forgive my heart
for letting itself become so vulnerable
to someone who had little to offer.

I had to have a self-check
& wipe my own tears,
because I couldn't quite believe
I allowed this to happen.

It took me awhile;
it still hurts now.
But one day I'll look back & say

It was meant to be this way.

Run Me The Details

"Everything Happens For A Reason" they say.
But what was the reason for all this destruction
that I neither caused nor deserved?

Every Time I'm With You I Feel As One

We haven't hung out or spoken in a while,
so, it's a little awkward when we decide to hang again.

At first, I'm short, answering every question & looking away
trying to act like I haven't missed him every single day.

The night goes on & I feel the old feelings turning back on.
Next minute I'm tangled in his arms listening to that lovely
heart.

Screaming *why* in my head but screaming *yes* in my heart.
Thinking "Wow love, you really know how to make me fall
for you all over again."

This happens every time we link up & say that it's just a
friendship, knowing very well that what we have is
something weird,

but it feels so special.

Our World, Our Everyday, Our Sad Reality

Everything that used to be so precious
& upheld with the most honor,
has now become corrupted & disintegrated.
Everything is ACCEPTED & nothing is RESPECTED.

It's Up To You

I can barely hear what you're saying
with that blunt between your lips,
Can't really see your facial expressions
through all this smoke & filth.
I hold your hand, you kiss my cheek,
the music's loud, I can barely breathe.

I don't mind, I'll stay a little longer,
just cause these vibes are growing & getting stronger.
Baby just put that blunt down;
look at me & follow my lead.
I can get you high
without the weed.

If you follow me,
you'll learn that I'm all you could possibly need.
Pick and choose,
me or the weed.

You could enjoy something temporary

or spend eternity with me.

I Can Still See Colors

I've been going through a lot,
I don't know if you can tell
from the redness in my eyes.
I've been crying a lot;
I'm surprised that I'm not blind.

Why Am I Like This?

The good boys that tried to build with me,
that tried to show me how worthy I really am?

                                        I ran them off.

All for the sake of trying to leave enough room for you
in my heart,

Just in case you decided to come back

                                        & stay.

I ran them off trying to keep you interested
& keep your attention.

                            You paid me none

& continued to live your life.

With or without me,
I could tell that you were doing perfectly fine.

            You were totally cool with ignoring me.

Not Bougie, Just Appreciative Of Who I've Become

Don't ever fill your heart with hate
all because I grew up to be someone more flattering.

I spent a lot of time dealing with my self-hatred
& the way I think.

I finally embraced that I am who I am,
& that will stay that way.

I changed the direction of my thoughts,
so that my body would align with my inner grace.

Before you say,
"she's selfish & full of herself,"
know that I worked to get to this point.
I deserve to, and will, flaunt my new mind & heart.

Teach & Show Me

I want to accept love
& learn how to dish it out properly.

Pain? What's That?

My pain tolerance is high,
no wonder why
I keep letting you back in my life.

The One I Wanted OBVIOUSLY Didn't Want Me

I push people away
because the one *I wanted* pushed *me* away.

It isn't right,
it isn't fair.

Tell me,
how can you accept the fact
that the one you wanted doesn't want you?
How does it never seem to wear on you?

It never seems to wear off
the memories,
the pain,
the tears,
the years,
our laughter
ringing in my ears.

This pain finds me in my happiest of years.
I've had to swallow A L O T of big pills.

I just want peaceful, mutual love,
that lovely balance.

You Made Me Glow

I'm so fickle minded when it comes to moving on
                                    or choosing you.
I know what you bring to the table & believe me
it's never enough.
You always leave me starving, in need of your love.
I know what's right & all of what's wrong.
But sometimes you're the only person I want to love on.
Your presence sets my heart alight.
Your voice rests sweetly upon my ears.
& your face?
Your face awakens the best parts of me,
parts of me that I've never even seen.

Feelings Are Dangerous

I see your potential
BUT,
dealing with you would only leave me in a sea of pain.

You've cluttered my brain;
I have no room to think.

This has been one of the worst experiences of my life.

I wish I never met you,
but then that would be a huge fib.
Maybe I hate the fact I fell for you,
but then again, I loved the way you made me feel.
I'm curious about how I was before I met you.
Was I happy?
Was I so worried?
Did I even know feelings existed?

I've been in this so long
I can't remember what it feels like to truly move on & say

F this.

Forever Alone

I tend to shove people away,
because I *love* my

S P A C E.

Then I wonder why I end up

lonely,

with tears stains on my face.

Far Behind Or On Time?

Sometimes
I feel like time is getting away from me.
Other times
I feel I'm exactly where I'm supposed to be.

2016 Phase

I feel everything deeply
& remember everything that anyone has ever said to me
I do not understand the feelings I've been feeling
for the past two years
No one I talk to has the right explanation
one that makes a light bulb click on in my brain

I'm sad,
drained,
& just want to rest.

Yet,
I'm so restless.

Peace,
I need Peace.

Excuse Me, I'm An Emotional Wreck Right Now

Don't get too attached to me.

Well at that point, it was too late.
I was vulnerable.
I just needed a hug.
Anyone's hands within mine
felt right.

But when reality sunk in,
it was a twisted-up situation.

I realized that I'd awoken someone's feelings
with no intent to feel for them
how they felt for me.

I just needed some temporary affection.
It's a big mess now.

That's what happens when you react from feelings.
You do things to speed the healing.
It didn't help me heal,
it only caused more destruction
& left a deeper scar
that hurts to peel.

Shut Up, No One Asked You For Your Opinions

NO!
Don't tell me
what I AM & AM NOT
for I know that
I am more than enough.

I Made It, I Did It

There's nothing like waking up from a long night,
smelling the residue of incense
burnt the night before,
tear stains dried on your favorite big T-Shirt,
with messy bed hair.
Yawning while thinking
I made it through another long, tough night alone.

Rehab I'm On The Way ... Maybe

I thought you were permanent.
Instead you were only my temporary high
& I became addicted.

I wish I would've figured this out sooner

Smh

I've gotten so many NO's
I've forgotten the joy
in what it feels like
to hear someone say
YES.

Seeking Euphoric Feels

I want to smile, not to keep from crying
but because I'm genuinely & truly HAPPY.

Why? What Was Your Purpose In Doing This To Me?

Trying to make sense of it all,
how do you go from cuddling one night,
to not even answering my calls?
This logic I can't digest has made me a complete mess.
Ever since I met you my heart has been in distress.

Don't Take It Personally, You Can If You Want To Though

I'm sorry for being standoffish
I'm just *FED UP*
with this nonsense.

It Was Always Just You, Never We

I only like when *you* hold me
I only like when *you* kiss my cheek repeatedly
I only like when *you* look in my eyes
I only like when *you* say my name wrong
"Jewells" instead of "Jewell"
I only love *your* presence
I only love *your* sense of humor
all I ever wanted was YOU

The Me You See, That's Who I Want To Be

I know I'm
difficult,
different,
a bit deceiving,
& can be a little down
but I promise if you have patience with me,
I'm worth keeping around.

When I love, I open up my all.
& that's how I fall,
until I have nothing left at all.
My heart is too big
I kind of wish it was hal/ved.

This pain that I've endured feels like it's here to last.
This pain in my eyes, this hole in my heart.
This crack in my brain keeps me shivering in the dark,
awake & blue,
leaning towards my solitude.

I'm ready to understand life
& receive all of its beautiful blessings.

I want to feel free, alive, without any more stressing.

The Good Girls Go Through The Worst

I can't help that I saw the universe in you
I can't help that I spoke you into my future
only to be placed in your past
I can't help that I knew your potential
& tried to get you to see it too.
I can't help that I was too in to you.

That's what girls like me do when we have big hearts.
We keep trying until our tries die out.
We keep breathing even if our last breath is for our lover.
It's girls like me, that get displaced
& put on a shelf to collect dust, pain, agony, filth,
while left blaming ourselves.

How Selfish Of You

I just wanted to show you
the abundance of love
the universe neglected to show.
You chose the universal suggestion of love
instead of my pure love.
I lost you that way.

You vs Him vs Me vs My Thoughts vs My Emotions

The more you want me, the more I want him...
I feel bad because I'm only leading you on.
I know that this is wrong,
but I just needed someone to love on.
I can't stop thinking about him
& the way his smile lit up my distorted world
& how refreshing it felt when he looked at me
as if I was all he'd ever need.
Even though he's bad for me & will never be what I hoped,
I have to tell the truth & keep it real.
You're a *nice guy* but its him I truly feel.

The Marks You Left

Your fingerprints are imprinted on me,
I still feel the indentions.
Your voice is the only sound I hear.
Holding your hands was the only way I stayed balanced.

Still feeling the remaining feelings
trying to overcome this challenge.
While rebuilding myself
it always feels like something is missing.

My heart aches for you,
I'm stuck here reminiscing.
I wanted forever,
but you never wanted to listen.

Somehow you became my biggest enemy
I can't live with this.

Was this your secret way
of being my worst distraction?
'Cause love this has taken my mind
on a whole other abstraction.

Ignore Your Emotions & Choose YOURSELF

I think us good girls have chosen a bad boy over a good boy at least once in our lives. For some reason they're the ones with the sweetest words, the softest touch & the brightest vibes.

Until they reel you in & captivate you...

Then they abuse you mentally, break you emotionally, & leave you wondering why. Stuck with a butt load of memories that replay in your head from early morning to late night.

Only then is when we realize that bad boys are considered BAD BOYS for a reason.

You can't play with a bad boy & expect a good outcome. Don't be that girl, know your worth and value. You're worth more than diamonds, rubies, & jewels put together.

You hold the light in your very own SELF. It's not too late.

Next time he tries to come back, let him know that his presence is no longer needed. Belittle him & leave him in deep thoughts of regret.

Yes, This is Definitely About You

We weren't in a relationship,
we never kissed, well only the one you offered on my cheek.
All we did was cuddle, talk, laugh, hang out
& play with each other's emotions.

Somehow in the midst of all that I fell for you,
but never told you the truth of how I really felt.
When I built up the courage to tell you
you asked, "What are your intentions with me?"

I replied, "To build with you, but over the past two years,
I can tell that you don't want that from me."
The only thing that you felt was applicable to say was "Oh."

Only then did I realize
you truly never gave a damn about me.
It was all a "I just want to see if she'll have sex with me & I'll
call it quits after that" type of game.
You never cared, you never wanted to build & grow with me.

You only saw me as a girl that you *thought* you were going
to use for selfish pleasures.
Gladly, I never allowed that to happen.

I never gave you that vibe that I was the type
to just allow any & everyone to use me up
& toss me to the curb,
as if I wasn't worthy enough to commit to

Why were you so comfortable
putting me in that low-class category?

That's low-down man.

#Disgusted

Please, Understand

Sorry if I push you away
& make you feel like your efforts aren't good enough.
It's totally unintentional
my heart is currently stuck on someone
who will never have the same feelings for me
who will never feel the need to commit to just *me.*

Excuse my emotional issues & my fickle minded heart.
I want to give him up
but a part of me wants him to stay.
I can't get his touch & face out of my brain.
My emotions are unbalanced.
I hope that one day they align.
These memories have a hold on me.

Dear past,

LEAVE ME ALONE, I WANT TO MOVE ON!

Sometimes I Want To Forget

For the last past few years,
I've been having nothing but mental wars
I can't remember what it feels like to not overthink.
To relax & forget that the world even exists.

This is Insane

Like a dreamy night & stormy rain
you once held me
& made me feel like everything was put together,
while cutting away my common sense.
I fell for the lies, the games,
the affection that you barely showed.
To this day,
I can't fathom why
I'm still not over you yet.

It Was All Lies

You have an ugly heart & a dark soul.
But your eyes were pure like heaven
& your words were as gentle as your touch.
Who wouldn't accidentally fall
for someone like You?

We Are Truly Different In Many Ways

I think it's amazing how God gave everybody a set of eyes,
but some see deeper than others.
Someone can meet you for the first time
& see that you're all they'll ever need.
Others can meet you & see & feel nothing.

KARMA, Do Your Job Love

I hurt, I shouted, I bled out for you;
you did nothing.

I had to stitch up my own wounds that you left so deep
I had to soothe my own mind that you left so confused
I had to release the feelings that I had bottled up for you.

It was all a game to you,
I love how you gave me up so easily,
how you talked about me to your home boys
as if I didn't spark not one flame in your heart,
having you thinking,
"Wow, she could be the one."

You are one pathetic, disgusting human being
& I hope you reap what you sow.
I hope you'll one day experience
all the hurt that you put me through.
Only then will the tables turn.
Only then will you hurt, shout & bleed for me.

But by then
I hope it's too late,
I hope I'm famous & living my best, happy life
while you're down here with regrets.

I don't wish the worst on others
but I do believe that everyone
deserves a taste of their own medicine.

You Can Love Helping, But You Can't Help Everyone

It's hard to give up on a person
when you see so much potential
You're persistently trying to better them,
to open their mind & ears.
Even if it's shredding your wellbeing into pieces,
even if your patience is wearing thin and well worn.
You keep trying
You'd rather help them understand their purpose & worth
rather than leaving them lost & confused.

The Unsaid Goodbye

You'll look for me in every girl you meet, but that will never happen, sorry love, there's only one me.

I gave you the chance, I gave you many chances to value my heart, to feel my expressions. You pushed me away, you failed to stay.

Many times, you placed tears upon my face. It was your lack of love, your lack of care that made me dark & made things fall apart.

You had me stuck, addicted to your touch. My sickened heart & blurry eyes, you continued to lie & play me as if I wasn't kind.

Your lies, your eyes, your addictive words carved in my brain stuck with me for days. It's been two years going on three. I let you come in & captivate me.

My love, I believe this is it. The time has finally come. The love I had for you is slowly fading away. Yes, it hurts, indeed I cry, but darling you failed to provide the love that I needed to survive.

I'll see you around, I'll hear about you too. But you will no longer be the one making my heart turn blue. The laughs & late nights watching movies till midnight, are all things of the past.

I've got to let go of this so that I can be free & find some new arms to hold me. I tried to wake you up from your stubborn dream, but you failed to realize the you I see.

A little side of me will always care, the only difference now is that I won't be there. By your side cuddled up, feeling warm, your arms around me feeling loved.

My love, you're no longer my love. For your touch is no longer a touch that I need.

I love you, but I've gotta choose *me*.

Just Going With The Flow

Sometimes that's what happens in life,
you don't try to figure it out anymore.
You don't say much, you don't feel the need
to explain in detail anymore.
You just live, hoping change is coming your way.

Just Want To Stay Found

Not being able to understand what level you're on
& what's your next step in life
is a huge, hard pill to swallow.
I'm forced to walk by faith,
not saying there's something wrong with that.
I'm just tired of being lost,
then found.

Only to remain lost again.

On 1/28/17 – The 3rd Time I've Seen You At A Party

A part of me is never going to let go of you & your vibes.

Your presence always consumes me. Sometimes I feel like It's the only thing keeping me going in life.

The more I see you, the weaker & deeper I feel for you. It's like your presence haunts me. Even when I'm out having fun trying to get the thought of you out of my broken mind, you appear at my location.

That night I saw you at the party I wanted to run in your arms & hug for the whole night. But instead when you tapped me on my shoulder, I turned around, with a slight smile & waved gently. Silently in my head saying, "I've been missing you like crazy, I need you now & kind of like forever, after the party let's hang & chill."

How am I supposed to get over you when you are everywhere?! This is one of the saddest things I've ever experienced. All in hopes that you'll hit me up tomorrow, sadly I know that won't happen.

& I miss you for the (billionth time).

Where Did The World Go Wrong?

We live in a world where good is good
but never enough.
Where pretty is perfection,
so being natural is a little tough.
Where butts & boobs are the only things to prove,
if you don't have a body like an hourglass,
they sleep on you.
Instead of a good personality and high class
they only focus on looks & that's sad.

A Note To Self

Shine my little star,
for this is not the end.

Waiting & Waiting & Waiting & ...

Knowing that you won't,
but still hoping that you will

The Truth

I'd rather fall off & evolve,
than fall off & be lost

Damn, I Fall For It Every Time

I ignored my intuition & ended up giving
you another entrance to slip into my heart

Isn't This A Great Feeling To Feel?

Seeing how well put together everyone else is,
only reminds me of how much I've fallen apart

Where Did The World Go Wrong? – Part 2

We live in a "I want it now or never" type of world.
A self-pursuing, inconsistent world.
No one wants to wait for anything.
Everything is rushed &
there's no such thing as patience or trust.

LOL, Truly Laughing OUT LOUD

So sad how the ones that put everyone first
always get put last.

How we're always there for everyone
but no one is there for us.

We're always willing to pick up the pieces of someone else,
carrying the weight of their worries.
But when we need help,
drowning in our own tears,
no one is ever there to wipe our eyes.

Isn't funny how the givers that give their all
get nothing in return?

Some Things Shouldn't Be In Our Control

You pick & choose who you want to keep & lose.
You pick & choose who you want to hold on to
or let go of.
Sometimes that's the problem
when decisions are left up to us,
we hold on to those who are destroying us
& let go of those who are trying to heal us.

Don't Hide It

Talk to me in such a way that is beyond my own intellect,
I wanna learn from you, I wanna learn someone new.
I like the challenge.
Introduce me to a vibe that I've never felt before.
A vibe that I never would have imagined.

Just One Of Those Nights

Staring at the stars,
Smiling with tears in my eyes.

Yay, I'm Doing It

You were like a drug,
I can finally say I've been
FIVE MONTHS CLEAN FROM YOU!!!!

We're Never On The Same Page

You became my everything
I became your nothing

Questions That I'll Never Know The Answers To

Trying to make sense of it all,
how do you continue to fall
for someone whose intention
isn't to catch you at all?

Mentally Over You

Our relationship is like an ink pen, it comes & goes.
It works sometimes & other times,
it stops working altogether.
It leaves scratches & tears all over the paper,
the paper in my mind
with all the memories that I have upheld for days, weeks,
months, years.
I'm ready to burn these pages of you
 & start a fresh new book.
 But how can I when you still exist?

You Were Nothing But A Waste Of Energy & Time

I wish you never would've messed everything up
I wouldn't be dealing with these nonsense
emotional ass emotions

Late Nights, Lantern Nights

I was planning on going to the lake tonight
to light a lantern
I forgot it needs two people
one to hold the lantern & one to light it
I forgot we don't talk anymore
I forgot that we no longer hang anymore
I forgot to forget about the memories with you.

Why You Gotta Be Like That?

I always tell myself one more time with you
& that'll be enough.
Truth be told its never enough.
The more you shun me,
the more I want you to stay.
You're so addictive I feel like you're a drug.

Someone Give Me The Secret Formula To Success

I've tried to do the whole
"Don't worry about it, just live, be care free,
meet new people, go after your dreams, be fearless."
But I always end up either where I started
or 10,000 steps backwards.
I feel like it's a losing situation, I try, I cry, & get nowhere.

Pay Attention To My Words

You'll know when things are still bothering me
I talk about them constantly.

Shhhhhh ...

You've always been my secret heartbreak.
I've always been too afraid to say...
I always played it off because I knew,
this was all game ... at least to you it was.

They Always Sleep On The Good Quiet Girls

I'm not your average teenager. I didn't have a date when I went to prom. I took my sister instead ... **both times**. I was a very stand-offish individual that felt more comfortable in solitude than with other human beings. It may sound weird but that's just how I flow.

If I take the time out to open up to you & show you my happy place, please honor that & don't destroy me or try to take that away. I stepped out of my bubble, my little world, all because I saw something in you that you haven't found in yourself, something that made me wonder and caught my attention.

Don't take advantage, don't take me for granted. Don't do something stupid to make me regret it. It's a privilege to have my attention. You don't see it now, but one day you'll get it.

I'll leave you with a thirst you can't quench yourself & you won't understand 'because you never took the time out to listen. Be careful how you treat the quiet caring females.
Those are the ones that have more to offer if you're willing to dig a little deeper, go a little farther, wait a little longer & put forth a little more effort.

We're the ones, we're the **true** keepers.

February 19, 2017

Remember that last night we were together?
You held me close,
closer than ever while I laid in your arms,
Why did it feel like it was the last time?
We were holding onto each other for dear life,
not wanting to detach.
Why did it feel like
that was going to be my last time feeling you?
Turns out that feeling was true.
Now I only see you on social media,
sometimes in my memories too.

(I Hope You Read This)

Thinking, Overthinking About YOU

I always ask myself what it would be like
if I just got one more chance to hang out with you.
How would I act?
What would I say?
What would I wear?

Would I cherish that moment,
or treat it like it's a "whatever" thing?
Would I want to hold your hand
& listen to the wind
like I used to do way back in 2016?
Would I still feel comfortable laying in your arms
even after you've ignored me for this long?

Something about you keeps my brain curiously wondering.
You're bad for me that's clear to say,
but sometimes I want to know if things would be the same.
I don't know when I'll let this fictional story
with made up lies & scenarios that did,
but most likely won't
happen again, go

I wonder what it would be like now,
since I know how you flow?
Maybe it's me just thinking & being me.
Maybe it's me overthinking,
you know that's my specialty.

Indeed, I Am The One

You treated me as if I wasn't worthy enough
as if my glow in the dark wasn't bright enough.
I've come to tell you that you're wrong,
your way of thinking is so far gone.
I'm brighter than the sun, moon & stars put together.
I'm brighter than a grill with a million diamonds.
I'm purer than the ocean waves that come ashore.
You're wrong for allowing yourself to disintegrate someone
so valuable.
Grow mentally before deciding if someone is really the one.

To Be Continued...

I know majority of my poems may seem sad,
but somehow my life just came down to that
wrapped in darkness,
no peak hole,
just heartless.

I kicked & screamed but no one ever heard me.
I stitched up my own wounds & healed.

I had to face reality,
there was NO ONE there helping me face this tragedy.
My heart, mind & soul ached,
but instead of going insane,
I forced myself to cope with the pain.

These eyes have witnessed it all,
how a person can be so broken,
but came out whole, beautiful, and strong.

I'll be honest,
lately I haven't been me,
but give me some time,
I'm just elevating to a better me.

The me you see is only temporary.

#StayTuned

I AM LEGENDARY

About the Author

Jewell Coleman is a singer/songwriter from Nashville, TN that not only loves to sing but also found herself loving poetry. Poetry has always been the quickest way for her to release the emotions & thoughts that were haunting her. Outside of singing & song writing, poetry started being a part of her everyday life, especially when things in her life started falling apart. She's been writing since middle school but kept it a secret until now, with her debut poetry collection "All My Random Thoughts in a Book."

Jewell graduated high school in 2016 but decided to not attend college because she wanted to pursue her different talents & dreams fully.

This book holds all her closely held experiences that have shaped her and are helping her transition into the young woman she is becoming and desires to be.

While she's on this journey, connect and grow with her by following her on Instagram @itsjewellbabe.

Made in USA - Kendallville, IN
48828_9781732712119
11 02 2022 1334